WE SHALL OVERCOME

FREEDOM RIDERS

A PRIMARY SOURCE EXPLORATION OF THE STRUGGLE FOR RACIAL JUSTICE

by Heather E. Schwartz

Consultant:
Bruce Allen Murphy, PhD
Fred Morgan Kirby Professor of Civil Rights
Lafayette College
Easton, Pennsylvania

CAPSTONE PRESS
a capstone imprint

Fact Finders Books are published by Capstone Press,
1710 Roe Crest Drive, North Mankato, Minnesota 56003
www.capstonepub.com

Library of Congress Cataloging-in-Publication Data
Schwartz, Heather E.
Freedom riders : a primary source exploration of the battle for racial justice / by Heather E. Schwartz.
pages cm. (Fact finders. We shall overcome.)
Includes bibliographical references and index.
Summary: "Uses primary sources to tell the story of the Freedom Riders during the U.S. Civil Rights
Movement"— Provided by publisher.
ISBN 978-1-4914-0222-1 (library binding) — ISBN 978-1-4914-0231-3 (paperback) —
ISBN 978-1-4914-0227-6 (eBook PDF)
1. African Americans—Civil rights—Southern States—History—Sources—Juvenile literature. 2. Civil rights
movements—Southern States—History—20th century—Sources—Juvenile literature. 3. Southern States—Race
relations—History—Sources—Juvenile literature. I. Title.
E185.61.S396 2015
323.1196'07307509045—dc23

2014002375

Editorial Credits
Jennifer Besel, editor; Cynthia Akiyoshi, designer; Wanda Winch, media researcher;
    Charmaine Whitman, production specialist

Photo Credits
AP Images, 19, 28, Ferd Kaufman, 25; Corbis: Bettmann, 11 (bottom), 13, 18; Courtesy Johnson Publishing Company,
LLC. All rights reserved, 9; Courtesy of Arkansas Democrat-Gazette, cover (background); Getty Images Inc: Time
& Life Pictures/Paul Schutzer, cover, Time Life Pictures/Joseph Scherschel, 21; Landov: Birmingham News, 16, 17,
Birmingham News/Ed Jones, 11 (top); Library of Congress: Prints and Photographs Division, 5, 6, 29; Mississippi
Department of Archives and History: Mississippi State Sovereignty Commission, 23 (all), Archives and Records
Services Division/The Clarion-Ledger, 22, Jackson Daily News, 27; Nashville Public Library Special Collections
Division, 15; Shutterstock: Olga k, paper background, Picsfive, paper pieces

Printed in the United States of America in Stevens Point, Wisconsin.
032014   008092WZF14

TABLE OF CONTENTS

A NOTE ABOUT PRIMARY SOURCES

Primary sources are newspaper articles, photographs, speeches, or other documents that were created during an event. They are great ways to see how people spoke and felt during that time. You'll find primary sources from the time of the Freedom Riders throughout this book. Within the text, primary source quotations are colored blue and set in italic type.

Chapter One

A MOB ATTACK

It was Mother's Day, 1961. A Greyhound bus carrying African-American and white passengers in Alabama came to a screeching halt. A mob of around 50 people surrounded the bus, hurling rocks and bricks through the windows. Carrying axes and pipes, the mob slashed the bus' tires. Someone threw a firebomb through a broken window. The protesters screamed, *"Burn them alive."* As black smoke filled the bus, Genevieve Hughes, a rider inside the bus, panicked. *"Oh, my God, they're going to burn us up!"* Then the fuel tank exploded, turning the bus into a fiery furnace. The Riders struggled to escape. The mob beat them with bats as they tried to flee.

The mob that May day was made up of angry white protesters. The protesters had stopped a bus carrying Freedom Riders.

In 1946 the Supreme Court ruled that **interstate** travel could not be **segregated**. But few police were making sure that black travelers had the same rights as whites. Freedom Riders were volunteers who rode buses that went between states to draw attention to the problem. But their peaceful rides soon turned into bloody battles.

▶ Photographer Joe Postiglione captured the scene outside Anniston, Alabama, as the Greyhound bus full of Freedom Riders was bombed.

interstate—connecting or between two or more states

segregate—to keep people of different races apart in schools and other public places

5

Chapter Two

CHALLENGING THE SEGREGATED SOUTH

By 1960 black and white Americans had lived separately in the South for almost 100 years. Jim Crow laws prevented blacks and whites from attending the same schools, using the same public restrooms, or even drinking from the same fountains. *"They did everything they could to make you feel inferior,"* recalled Kenneth Young, a black man who grew up in the segregated South. *"They didn't miss a trick. If they had two fountains they'd put another cup up there for the blacks."*

▶ Throughout the South, including this streetcar terminal in Oklahoma City, Oklahoma, African-Americans were forced to use facilities labeled "colored."

Who Was Jim Crow?

Many of the people who supported Jim Crow laws felt African-Americans were not as smart as white people. In 1957 William F. Buckley, editor of the *National Review*, wrote about whether whites should rule over blacks. *"The sobering answer is Yes—the White community is so entitled because, for the time being, it is the advanced race."*

In the early 1800s, a white performer created a black character called Jim Crow. As Jim Crow, the performer made fun of African-Americans. The foolish character's name later came to be used to describe segregation laws.

Not all people supported segregation, though. These people—both black and white—worked to end it. In 1946 and again in 1960, African-Americans won landmark Supreme Court cases. In the case of *Morgan v. Virginia*, the Court banned segregation on interstate buses. Then 14 years later, in *Boynton v. Virginia*, it banned segregation in waiting rooms, restrooms, and lunch counters for interstate travelers. The problem was that these rulings were almost completely ignored in the South.

The Freedom Riders

It was obvious that Southern states were doing nothing to enforce the Supreme Court rulings. So James Farmer, director of the Congress of Racial Equality (CORE), decided to do something about it. In May 1961 Farmer organized the Freedom Rides. CORE recruited protesters to ride two regularly scheduled buses across states in the **Deep South**.

On the buses black and white Freedom Riders would sit together even if they were told to sit separately. At bus stations, they would try to eat together. They would disobey signs directing them to "colored" and "white" waiting rooms.

The Riders knew people might insult or even attack them. *"There is a possibility that we will not be served at some stops. There is a possibility that we might be arrested. This is the only trouble that I anticipate,"* Freedom Rider Genevieve Hughes told a reporter before leaving.

Deep South—the states of Alabama, Georgia, Louisiana, Mississippi, and Tennessee

But under no circumstances were the Riders allowed to use violence. *"... I was concerned with finding nonviolent solutions to violent conflict ..."* Farmer said in an interview later in life. In preparation for the rides, the volunteers were trained to react calmly to insults. They practiced not fighting back when attacked. The Riders were willing to put themselves in danger. They were determined to draw attention to states that were ignoring the law and getting away with it.

▶ some of the original Freedom Riders:
back row (left to right): John Lewis, Jim Peck, Ed Blankenheim, Hank Thomas, Walter Bergman, James Farmer
front row (left to right): Joe Perkins, Charles Person, Frances Bergman, Genevieve Hughes, Jimmy MacDonald

Chapter Three
THE FIRST RIDERS SET OUT

On May 4, 1961, the Freedom Riders left from Washington, D.C., and planned to ride to New Orleans. *"Boarding that Greyhound bus to travel through the heart of the Deep South, I felt good,"* Freedom Rider John Lewis recalled years later. *"I felt happy. I felt liberated. I was like a soldier in a nonviolent army. I was ready."*

When they got to Atlanta, the Freedom Riders met the Rev. Dr. Martin Luther King Jr. He was a major leader of the civil rights movement. The Freedom Riders were excited. They hoped he'd ride with them. Instead, he encouraged them to turn back before they reached Alabama.

Trailblazers

The Freedom Riders weren't the first activists to test the 1946 Supreme Court ruling. In April 1947, 16 people held the Journey of Reconciliation. Black riders rode in the front of the bus, while white riders sat in the back. *"As a result of the Journey of Reconciliation a number of black[s] and whites were jailed,"* recalled Bayard Rustin, a CORE founder who led the ride. The Journey didn't stop segregation, but it paved the way for the next wave of riders.

lynch—to be put to death, often by hanging

▶ On May 15, 1961, the Freedom Riders waited at the Birmingham, Alabama, bus station. The day before, they had been attacked by a white mob.

King was worried about the Ku Klux Klan (KKK) in Alabama. The KKK was known for harassing and even **lynching** African-Americans who challenged Jim Crow laws. King worried the group would do the same to the Riders. *"You will never make it through Alabama,"* he told them. Despite King's warning the Riders pressed on.

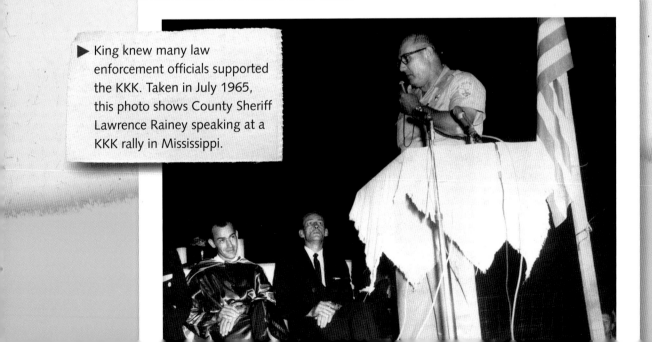

▶ King knew many law enforcement officials supported the KKK. Taken in July 1965, this photo shows County Sheriff Lawrence Rainey speaking at a KKK rally in Mississippi.

Mob Violence

From Atlanta the Freedom Riders left in two buses, one Greyhound and one Trailways. The Greyhound bus headed to Anniston, Alabama. When the bus reached Anniston, a mob of angry white men was waiting. The men were determined to kill the Freedom Riders. They punctured the bus' tires and broke its windows. They threw a bomb inside and blocked the door. *"The fuel tank exploded. I heard somebody say, 'It's gonna go, it's gonna go.' [The attackers] ran and that was the only way we could get that door open,"* recalled Freedom Rider Hank Thomas.

All the passengers eventually made it off the bus. Thirteen Riders were taken to a local hospital. But hospital employees were worried the mob would come there. So they ordered the Riders to leave as soon as possible.

FACT

Two undercover Alabama Highway Patrol agents were on the Greyhound bus. One wore a hidden microphone to eavesdrop on the Riders. No one in the mob knew the agents were on board. The agents were also trapped on the bus as it was lit on fire.

The Trailways bus headed to Birmingham, Alabama. Bull Connor, commissioner of public safety, made a deal with the KKK. Klan members could have 15 minutes to do whatever they wanted to the Freedom Riders before police would arrive.

The mob greeted Riders with fists and clubs. *"They knocked one man, a white man, down ... and they beat him and kicked him until his face was a bloody red pulp,"* said a reporter.

John Patterson, governor of Alabama, spoke in support of the way Freedom Riders were treated. *"... you just can't guarantee the safety of a fool, and that's what these folks are. Just fools."*

President John F. Kennedy was aware of the violence. He tried calling Patterson. But phone calls were the only actions Kennedy was willing to take ... yet.

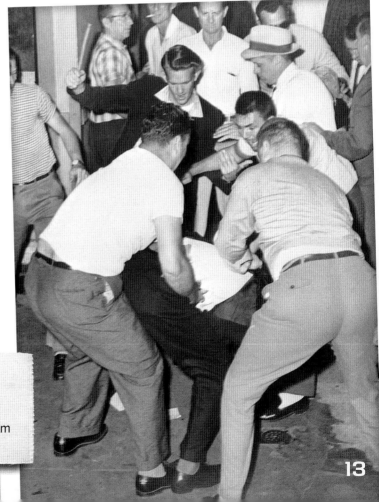

► On May 14, 1961, a mob of white men attacked the Freedom Riders at the Birmingham bus station.

Chapter Four
STUDENT RIDERS

Despite meeting with brutal violence, the CORE Freedom Riders decided to continue their rides. Drivers, however, were afraid to take them. The Freedom Riders were shaken too. In the end, they flew to New Orleans. Their Freedom Rides were over.

But in Nashville, Fisk University students were ready to act. Student Diane Nash had already helped **integrate** lunch counters in Nashville. Now she came forward to organize a second wave of Freedom Riders. *"It was critical that the Freedom Ride not stop, and that it be continued immediately,"* she said.

At that point, agreeing to go on a Freedom Ride was no easy decision. Students who volunteered knew they would face violence and might even be killed.

integrate—to bring people of different races together in schools and other public places

Still, students from several colleges wanted to go. Ten were selected to continue the ride from Birmingham to New Orleans. *"After we had talked it out and I was one of those chosen to go, I went back to my room and spent a lot of time reading the Bible and praying,"* recalled Freedom Rider Jim Zwerg. *"Because of what had happened in Birmingham and in Anniston ... none of us honestly expected to live through this."*

▶ Just one day after the attacks in Birmingham, Diane Nash (second from right) began organizing a second wave of Riders.

Bullied Out of Birmingham

On May 17, 1961, 10 student Freedom Riders left on a bus in Nashville headed for Birmingham. Connor was waiting for them at the Birmingham station. He let the regular passengers off the bus. Then he directed police officers to **intimidate** the Freedom Riders and make sure their story wouldn't get out to the public.

Police officers hid the Freedom Riders by covering the bus' windows with newspaper and cardboard. They made the Riders sit on the bus for two hours. Suffering in the heat, the activists had no idea what might happen to them. When they were finally allowed off the bus, they went to the whites-only section of the bus station. Right away, they were arrested.

▶ Police covered the bus' windows with cardboard. They told reporters they covered the windows to protect the Riders' safety.

intimidate—to threaten in order to force certain behavior

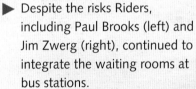

▶ Despite the risks Riders, including Paul Brooks (left) and Jim Zwerg (right), continued to integrate the waiting rooms at bus stations.

Later that night the Freedom Riders were taken out of their cells. Connor and other officers drove them to the Tennessee state line. Connor kicked them out of Alabama and told them to catch a train back to Nashville. *"Of course, I couldn't let Bull have the last word,"* recalled Freedom Rider Catherine Burks-Brooks. *"So I told him we would see him back in Birmingham by high noon."*

Riots Break Out

The Riders insisted on going back to Birmingham. When they got there, another nine student Riders were there too. They were all ready to continue to New Orleans, but no bus drivers would take them. Finally, police escorted them to Montgomery, Alabama. There, the Freedom Riders were on their own to face an angry mob.

As the only white man in the group, Jim Zwerg was quickly targeted. Someone punched him in the face and knocked him down. *"Another group of whites pressed in after Mr. Zwerg had fallen and pushed and stomped his face into the hot, tarry surface of the road,"* reported *The New York Times* on May 20, 1961.

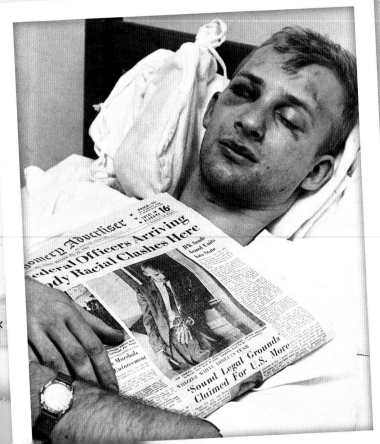

▶ Jim Zwerg after the attack

Many black Freedom Riders were attacked too. Police stood and watched while the activists were beaten nearly to death. Still, the Freedom Riders weren't willing to quit. *"These beatings cannot deter us from our purpose ... We want only equality and justice, and we will get it,"* Zwerg told a reporter the next day.

A few days after the riot, Patterson defended the mob's actions. *"[The Freedom Riders] are buying tickets from town to town and getting off in each town ... and pushing themselves onto people who are citizens of those communities in such a manner as to incense them and enrage them and to provoke them into acts of violence."*

FACT

John Siegenthaler was an assistant to U.S. Attorney General Robert Kennedy. He was sent to Alabama to help calm the violence. He was beaten and knocked out during the Montgomery riot.

19

Chapter Five

GAINING GROUND

On May 21, 1961, civil rights leaders held a rally to support the Freedom Riders. About 1,500 people gathered at the First Baptist Church in Montgomery.

But another crowd gathered outside the church. And this group was definitely not there to support desegregation. *"As the crowd grew in number— eventually as many as 3,000 people appeared— it also grew in vitriol and hostility. The crowd began hurling rocks and bricks through the stained-glass windows, and tear gas drifted through the sanctuary,"* recalled Freedom Rider Bernard Lafayette Jr.

With no way out of the church, Dr. King called U.S. Attorney General Robert Kennedy for help. *"... we must be sure that we adhere absolutely to nonviolence,"* King told the people in the church. *"Now it's very easy for us to get angry and bitter and even violent in a moment like this, but I think this is a testing point ... We can't do that. We have won the moral victory."*

They won more than a moral victory when federal troops came to rescue them. By taking action to protect the activists, the U.S. government upheld federal law over state law. It was a significant triumph for the Freedom Riders.

▶ Photographer Joseph Scherschel captured the fires started by rioters in Montgomery in May 1961.

Jailed in Mississippi

A few days after the church attack, the Freedom Riders prepared to leave for Jackson, Mississippi. James Farmer later spoke of his feelings that day. *"... the young Freedom Riders ... had joined forces in Montgomery to take the ride into Jackson, and I was there and they presumed I was going with ... but I had other thoughts ... the bottom line was that I was scared to death."*

When Riders arrived at the Jackson bus station, they tried to integrate the waiting rooms. Police arrested them. Many members of the local community were pleased.

▶ This editorial, printed in *The Clarion-Ledger* in Jackson, Mississippi, on May 28, 1961, showed how many people felt about the Freedom Riders.

Officers Did Good Job; Let Them Do It Again

(AN EDITORIAL)

Mississippians from the governor on down are proud of the manner in which our officers of state and city have handled the so - called "freedom riders" in our midst.

Reports say the second wave of misguided young people is on the way. Let's permit the officers of the law handle this group without hindrance.

If the new crop of CORE visitors tries to create a violent incident, let's do not be provoked by their unlawful acts into lawlessness of our own. Let's just let the officers show the invaders quietly to our jails.

This plan works out to defeat the whole program of the trouble-seekers. It is our best policy.

► Police took mug shots of each arrested Freedom Rider, including these of Riders (from top left to bottom right) Catherine Burks-Brooks, Jane Ellen Rosett, Ernest Patton Jr., Kenneth Shilman, Dion Tyrone Diamond, and Joan Trumpauer-Mulholland.

The Freedom Riders were sent to a famously tough prison known as Parchman. At the prison some Riders claimed that guards tortured them. *"Their clothes were ripped off of them,"* said Freedom Rider Kenneth Shilman in an article in the *Jackson Daily News*. *"As they were dragged past us, the skin was tearing off their bodies, and the extreme pain showed on their faces."* The article also included a response from Sheriff J. R. Gilfoy, denying any improper treatment. He said, *"We're leaning over backward in handling them."*

Continuing the Fight

The Freedom Riders were scared, but they didn't let it show. They sang in prison for hours every day. When they were ordered to stop, they sang louder. *"We did a lot of singing. And they didn't like the singing. Every time that they would threaten to do something, we would sing. For example, [they would say] 'We're going to take your mattress.' [We would sing], 'You can take our mattress, oh yes, ...'"* recalled Freedom Rider Ernest "Rip" Patton Jr. *"Now that meant sleeping on steel, but we were willing to give up those mattresses."*

Outside Parchman the battle continued. CORE sent out a national plea asking for more volunteers to ride into Jackson as Freedom Riders. Anyone who did would be arrested, but that was part of the plan. *"We wanted to fill up the jails and place as great a burden on the state as possible, for as long as we could,"* said James Farmer.

FACT

Many Freedom Riders also went on a hunger strike while in jail. The strike lasted for 12 days.

▶ Arrests like this one in a white waiting room at a bus station in Jackson, Mississippi, happened daily as Riders flooded the city.

From jail the Riders declared *"Jail No Bail."* Each rider decided to stay in jail for 39 days, which was the maximum time they could stay without losing their right to **appeal**. Then after 39 days they posted bond and filed their appeals saying their arrests were unconstitutional. Dragging out their time in jail kept their fight in the spotlight.

appeal—to ask another court to review a case already decided by a lower court

Chapter Six
THE IMPACT

In the summer of 1961, volunteer Freedom Riders came to Jackson from all over the country. *"I got up one morning in May and I said to my folks at home, 'I won't be back today because I'm a Freedom Rider,'"* recalled Pauline Knight-Ofosu. *"It was like a wave or wind that you didn't know where it was coming from or where it was going, but you knew you were supposed to be there."*

"We were past fear," recalled Freedom Rider Joan Trumpauer-Mulholland. *"If we were going to die, we were gonna die, but we can't stop."*

More than 300 Freedom Riders were arrested and sent to jail. They became a source of inspiration, causing others to stand up and fight for desegregation.

FACT

A total of 436 people rode interstate buses as Freedom Riders.

However, some people were just as passionate about keeping segregation in place. In June 1961 the *Jackson Daily News* published letters from readers who opposed integration.

READERS' VIEWPOINT

PLEASE SIGN YOUR NAME—KEEP LETTERS BRIEF

Flying U.S. Flag

Editor, Daily News — Are foreign ships permitted to fly the American flag? If so, which end do they fly it on—the bow or stern?

Respectfully yours,

F. Polk

Oakvale, Miss.

Editor's note: Our Navy researcher reports that foreign vessels may and do fly the American flag from the foremast while in United States ports. United States ships may and do fly the flag of the country they are visiting. You're welcome.

'Roosevelt Raiders'

Editor, Daily News — I noticed, in a letter printed in your edition of June 13, a suggestion to refer to the "freedom riders" as "Kennedy's Raiders." While this, I think, is an excellent suggestion, let us not allow all the facts to escape us.

A brief look into history will reveal that this sort of agitation originated in the vote-seeking actions of Franklin Roosevelt, and was pushed most energetically by she who, at the last Democratic Convention, was introduced as "the first lady of our land."

Aside from wondering to whose "land" this referred, I will close by offering the suggestion that it might be more appropriate to call the "freedom riders" "Roosevelt's Raiders."

Stephen H. Cole

650 NE 55th St.

Miami, Fla.

Winter Tourist

Editor, Daily News — In connection with all this racial business

Real Democracy In Action Is Needed

Editor, Daily News — I hope by this letter, to make it clear just how one American citizen feels about integration of Negroes with white persons. Two-thirds of the world's population is black and very prolific, and the white race has just one decision to make — for self preservation or complete extinction.

Six generations of my family have lived and died here, and I won't watch this black tide sweep over us without protest. We owe it to our children and grandchildren to see that it never happens, or there will be no future for future generations. The white race will have disappeared from the face of the earth!

Right now, we should remember what Abraham Lincoln had to say about mixing the white and black races. In a Charleston, Ill., speech in 1858, these were his words:

"I will say then, that I am not nor ever have been in favor of bringing about the social and political equality of the white and black race ... ever have ... ing voters ... nor of qua ... fice, nor t ... people; a ... tion to th ... cal differ ... and black ... will forev ... living to ... cial and ... asmuch ... while th ... there mu ... ior and ... as any ... having ... signed

...spect for others and our Southern states, they would put some of the money wasted on bus rides to a good use in gifts for the little ones in orphan homes, hospitals and institutions. They could have made someone happy.

Get on your knees and thank God for what you have. I am not able to afford even a radio, but I look at some of my neighbors and am thankful—A boy and a girl both blind and paralyzed from childhood, now ages 27 and 32.

God did not promise anything but bread and water. You all have good schools, churches and colleges, your own business. Your children won't learn anymore in our schools than they will in yours.

If God had wanted to mix people he would have made them the same color. You are not going to always be in this world. You had better be worrying about where you are going to sit in the next world, rather than where you can sit on the bus today.

Hang your head in shame and look at the veterans in hospitals without arms, legs or sight, God has given you all these, but you are using them to stir up trouble.

The back end of the bus gets to town at the same time the front end does.

supply — ski ... ories from F ... pens who are ... terested in "H ... in the raking ... to the level o ...

Yes, you hav ... pathy of all t ... but, as is know ... ends of the ea ... good will are s ... sympathy too, ... are smitten da ... nonsense of c ... those who are ... when not on a p ...

Yours si ...

Marvin C ...

Decatur, ...

Whose D ... Need Cle ...

Editor, Daily ... a reply to F. ... on Southland. ...

Ordinarily th ... son of your qu ... do not deserve ... answer; howeve ... our donkey in ... me to reply. ...

Your attack ... the South see ... til the North h ... If the North's ... aired we will ... the stench. ...

I visited you ...

▶ The editorials give a good look at how deeply many Southerners wanted to keep life as it was. Mrs. E. J. Caldwell wrote, *"If God had wanted to mix people, he would have made them the same color."* Sarah Ringer's letter also shows the fear many felt over integration. *"... I won't watch this black tide sweep over us without protest. We owe it to our children and grandchildren to see that it never happens, or there will be no future for future generations."*

The End of Interstate Bus Segregation

On September 22, 1961, the battle officially ended. The Interstate Commerce Commission (ICC) outlawed segregation on buses traveling between states and in bus stations. Unlike what happened after the Supreme Court rulings, the ICC took steps to enforce the rules. Those who didn't obey were subject to penalties.

Later that fall the National Association for the Advancement of Colored People (NAACP) and CORE sent riders out as testers. They discovered many Southern states were obeying the new order. Black passengers were allowed to sit in the fronts of buses. At bus stations everyone could use the same restaurants and restrooms.

► The ICC ruling said all segregation signs had to come down by November 1, 1961. Taken on November 2, this photo captures McComb, Mississippi's, Police Chief George Guy refusing to take down the sign.

► Freedom Riders Henry Thomas (left) and Jim Peck (right) protested at a Trailways bus terminal in New York City on May 17, 1961, after being attacked in Birmingham days earlier.

Some Southern communities tried to keep their old way of life. Alabama Governor Patterson said that if the Freedom Riders *"continue to invade our state and continue to try to run over us, we want to serve notice that we are going to defend ourselves and we are not going to take it lying down."*

Eventually, however, the ICC rule led to more Supreme Court cases that struck down state segregation laws. Even those who resisted integration could not keep ignoring federal law. The Freedom Riders' major victory drew even more support for the civil rights movement and, eventually, helped outlaw segregation in the United States.

Selected Bibliography

"2 Beaten 'Riders' Dare Mob Death." *The Milwaukee Sentinel*, May 22, 1961. http://news.google.com/newspapers?nid=1368&dat=19610522&id=cdYpAAAAIBAJ&sjid=yRAEAAAAIBAJ&pg=4730,1248590

"The First Freedom Ride: Bayard Rustin on His Work with CORE." Columbia University Oral History Collection, September 12, 1985. http://historymatters.gmu.edu/d/6909/

"Freedom Riders' Jail Songs in Parchman Prison." Oprah's Tribute to Freedom Riders, May 4, 2011. http://www.oprah.com/oprahshow/Freedom-Riders-Jail-Songs-in-Parchman-Prison-Video

"Freedom Riders: Watch the Full Film." American Experience, 2010. http://www.pbs.org/wgbh/americanexperience/freedomriders/watch

"Freedom Rides." Digital Public Library of America. http://dp.la/exhibitions/exhibits/show/activism/civil-rights-actions/freedom-rides

"James Farmer: The Complete Interview." NPR Media Player, September 17, 1985. http://www.npr.org/2011/04/29/135836458/a-freedom-ride-organizer-on-non-violent-resistance

Lafayette, Bernard Jr. "The Siege of the Freedom Riders." *The New York Times*, May 19, 2011. http://www.nytimes.com/2011/05/20/opinion/20Lafayette.html?_r=2&

"Readers' Viewpoint." *Jackson Daily News*. June 22, 1961. http://www.freedomridersfoundation.org/images/photos-articles-artifacts/readers.viewpoint.06.22.61.jpg

"WSB-TV newsfilm clip of a press conference during which Alabama governor John Patterson condemns the Freedom Riders for instigating racial trouble and demands that the Freedom Riders and Martin Luther King, Jr. leave the state, Montgomery, Alabama, 1961 May 23." Digital Library of Georgia and Walter J. Brown Media Archives and Peabody Awards Collection, University of Georgia Libraries, 2007. http://crdl.usg.edu/do:ugabma_wsbn_34963

Glossary

appeal (uh-PEEL)—to ask another court to review a case already decided by a lower court

Deep South (DEEP SOUTH)—the states of Alabama, Georgia, Louisiana, Mississippi, and Tennessee

integrate (IN-tuh-grate)—to bring people of different races together in schools and other public places

interstate (in-tur-STATE)—connecting or between two or more states

intimidate (in-TIM-uh-date)—to threaten in order to force certain behavior

lynch (LYNCH)—to be put to death, often by hanging, by mob action and without legal authority

segregate (SEG-ruh-gate)—to keep people of different races apart in schools and other public places

Critical Thinking Using the Common Core

1. Compare the newspaper editorial on page 22 with the quotation from Kenneth Shilman on page 23. How does each person's point of view shape the way he or she talks about the Freedom Riders event? (Craft and Structure)

2. Rev. Dr. Martin Luther King Jr. told the Freedom Riders, "You will never make it through Alabama." What evidence did King have for making this statement? Use information from this book and other sources to support your answer. (Integration of Knowledge and Ideas)

Internet Sites

FactHound offers a safe, fun way to find Internet sites related to this book. All of the sites on FactHound have been researched by our staff.

Here's all you do:
Visit *www.facthound.com*
Type in this code: 9781491402221

Check out projects, games and lots more at
www.capstonekids.com

Index